THE
GHOSTLY TALES
OF
THE
HAUNTED
SOUTH

Published by Arcadia Children's Books
A Division of Arcadia Publishing
Charleston, SC
www.arcadiapublishing.com

Spooky America is a trademark of Arcadia Publishing, Inc.

First published 2021

Manufactured in the United States

ISBN: 978-1-4671-9840-0

Library of Congress Control Number: 2021938354

v

All images used courtesy of Shutterstock.com.

Spooky America

THE GHOSTLY TALES OF THE HAUNTED SOUTH

ALAN BROWN

Adapted from *The Haunted South* by Alan Brown

arcadia®
CHILDREN'S BOOKS

ATLANTIC OCEAN

GULF OF MEXICO

Table of Contents & Map Key

Introduction 2

1 Chapter 1. Alabama 7
  1 DAR House Museum
  2 USS Alabama
  3 Bay Minette Public Library

2 Chapter 2. Arkansas 19
  4 Harding University
  5 Site of Mayberry inn

3 Chapter 3. Florida 29
  6 The Historic Sacred Heart Hospital
  7 The Kenwood Inn

4 Chapter 4. Georgia 37
  8 Springer Opera House
  9 Fort Pulaski National Monument

5 Chapter 5. Kentucky 45
  10 Spurlington Tunnel
  11 Octagon Hall Museum

6 Chapter 6. Louisiana 51
  12 The Myrtles Plantation
  13 St. Louis Cemetery No. 1

7 Chapter 7. Mississippi 65
  14 Deer Island
  15 Rock and Roll Graveyard

8 Chapter 8. North Carolina 73
  16 Chimney Rock
  17 Biltmore Estate
  18 Devils' Tramping Ground

9 Chapter 9. South Carolina 81
  19 Abbeville Opera House
  20 The Leamington Lighthouse

10 Chapter 10. Tennessee 87
  21 Magnolia Manor
  22 Chapel Hill Ghost Lighthouse

11 Chapter 11. Virginia 97
  23 The Martha Washington Inn
  24 Fort Monroe

Chapter 12. Afterword 105

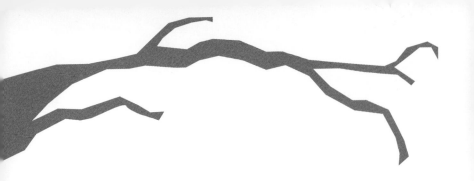

Introduction

When you think of the American South, what comes to mind? Maybe it's stories of the grand battles fought at the Alamo in San Antonio, Texas. You may also have learned about the American Civil War in school. In nearly every respect, the South has a rich cultural heritage and grand traditions.

But have you heard about all of the ghosts that haunt the South? If not, be prepared for the mystery and fright that awaits you in the following pages Some of these apparitions and phantoms have not kept up with the tradition of Southern hospitality!

The sixteen states that make up the southern United States have roots that date back to the eighteenth century. Cities like St. Augustine, Florida, and Jamestown, Virginia, have the distinction of being some of the oldest settlements in the United States—which is a lot of time to document supernatural activity.

When you think of ghosts, haunted houses normally come to mind. The South is famous for its haunted pre–American Civil War homes. The Myrtles, in St. Francisville, Louisiana, is known to house as many as seventeen ghosts within its dark hallways. A lesser-known haunted house in the South is the DAR (Daughters of the American Revolution) House in Mobile, Alabama. Most of the ghosts who haunt this house are the spirits of children. These little ghosts can be scary when they make objects move on their own. But most of the time, they are just pesky poltergeists.

Other haunted buildings can be found in the South, as well. The Sacred Heart Hospital in Pensacola, Florida, now houses a number of offices and small businesses—and a ghost that shows up as the spirit of a nun who it seems is still on the job! Many theaters in the South are believed to be haunted, too. These ghosts are the spirits of stage crew members who died accidentally while performing their duties. The Springer Opera House, in Columbus, Georgia, is haunted by the ghost of Edwin Booth, the brother of John Wilkes Booth. He stays there, people say, because of the warm reception the people of Columbus gave him when he performed *Hamlet* there.

Some Southern locations have simply acquired a haunted reputation by nature. Off the coast of Biloxi, Mississippi, is Deer Island, supposedly haunted by the ghost of a headless pirate who stands guard over buried treasure on the island. The Devil's Tramping Ground, in Chatham County, Virginia, is a barren circle forty feet in diameter. Nothing grows there because the Devil himself walked around in a circle centuries ago while trying to figure out new ways to trap human souls.

Well, that's what local legend says. But are any of these stories true?

Most legends have basis in fact, so *something* must have happened, right? You, the reader, must decide whether or not these tales are 100 percent true or the product of overactive imaginations.

Alabama

THE SMALL GHOSTS OF THE DAR HOUSE (MOBILE, ALABAMA)

In the mid-1800s, the life of a steamboat captain was very appealing for men who wanted to see the world and did not want to be tied down. One of these men, Captain Charles G. Richards from Maine, began to change his outlook on life after marrying Carline Elizabeth Steel in 1842. As their family grew, Captain Richards grew weary of the life of a roving riverboat man. After a few years of marriage, he moved his family to Mobile, where he set up shop as a dry goods merchant. The spacious house that he and his wife bought in 1860 was soon filled with the sounds of their ten children laughing and playing. As you can probably imagine, a house with ten children needs to be quite spacious so that everyone can be comfortable. Oftentimes, Captain Richards would ask his sons to play outside on the house porch, while his daughters played with toys and games of their own inside the house. Their happiness did not last long, however. The captain-turned-merchant was heartbroken when Caroline passed away giving birth to their eleventh child.

Fortunately, the historical integrity of Captain Richards's old house was maintained over time, and when the Daughters of the American Revolution (DAR) acquired the house in 1973, they converted it into a museum. Soon after, tourists reported hearing strange sounds, like the boisterous laughter of little kids and soft whispers at the top of the stairs; one of the Richards children's favorite places to play.

More and more visitors to the DAR building began talking about their mysterious encounters there. In 2007, a group of paranormal investigators was called upon to conduct experiments in search of any paranormal presence. In one of the bedrooms, they placed several marbles on the bed and asked the spirits to move them. Three minutes passed, and nothing happened, so the investigators then took a red marble, set it on the middle of the bed, and told the spirits they would leave the room if the marble moved. They sat by the bed, hoping the spirits would cooperate. Moments later, the red marble rolled a couple of inches—not very far, but at least it moved on its own. The joyful ghost hunters then left the house for an hour to celebrate.

But when they returned, the red marble was gone. According to those familiar with the story, the red marble remains missing to this day. And that's not the only creepy occurrence. Tour guides have reported hearing the raucous noises of little boys playing on the porch, though none can ever be seen or found.

Mary Ruth Andrews—a tour guide at the DAR—had a ghostly experience one evening

while she was closing up for the night. She walked into a room on the first floor and heard a banging so loud that it scared her half to death. The only thing in the room that was out of order was a candle that had tipped over, but she couldn't imagine how something so small could have made such a big racket.

Then, one morning, as Mary Ruth opened up the house for the day, she saw a strange man sitting on a sofa. She became alarmed, knowing very well that she would normally be the only one inside the house at that time in the morning. She did a double-take, but when she looked back at the sofa, the man was gone. At that moment, she realized she had probably seen a ghost! As she continued her day, she began to wonder if the apparition she saw on the sofa was the ghost of Captain Richards, and if it was his spirit who made such a racket on the first floor. This possibility shook Mary Ruth Andrews to her bones!

The ghost of an adult woman with blonde hair seems to be haunting the DAR House as well. One morning, one of the tour guides pulled her car up the driveway. She glanced up and saw a woman standing in a second-floor window. The tour guide wasn't concerned, because she thought it was another guide she was supposed to be working with that day. As she entered the house, she exclaimed, "I'm here!" However, she got a feeling of fright when no one answered. Suddenly, she heard a noise coming from the outside. She looked out the window and saw the other guide walking up to the front door. She rushed up to her and asked if she was the woman standing in the second-story window.

"No, I just got here," she said.

In a low, shaky voice, the tour guide replied, "I was afraid you'd say that."

A few of the tour guides believe the spirit of Caroline Richards is the female ghost that haunts the second floor of the house. Ghost hunters from the 2007 investigation surmised that Captain Richards often keeps his wife company on the second floor. Others think she has been seen staring out of the second floor window because she is looking for her children. Sometimes, a stern voice can be heard in the house when no one else is around, and many believe it is the voice of Caroline Richards, trying to keep her kids in line. Family drama never ends, even in the afterlife!

THE HAUNTED BATTLESHIP (MOBILE, ALABAMA)

The term "ghost" usually applies to people or, occasionally, even animals. But did you know ships can be ghostly, as well? One could even say the World War II–era battleship called the

USS *Alabama*, in Mobile, Alabama, is a "ghost ship" because it is said to be totally haunted!

The USS *Alabama* was christened on August 16, 1942. It was involved in some of the fiercest sea battles in World War II, including the Battle of Leyte Gulf on October 25, 1944. After riding out a typhoon in December 1944, the USS *Alabama* shot down two planes from the Japanese fleet on May 4, 1945. The "Mighty A," as it was known, was decommissioned on January 9, 1945. With the help of Alabama schoolchildren who raised over $100,000, the old battleship was saved from demolition in 1964. It was moved to its final resting place at the USS *Alabama* Battleship Memorial Park in Mobile.

During one unfortunate incident, eight sailors died as a result of "friendly fire"; a gun mount had accidentally fired on another gun mount nearby. Witnesses to the horrible scene said the USS *Alabama* was plastered with the bloody remains of the unfortunate sailors. It was said that all that was left of the gun commander was his boots.

Most of the ghostly activity aboard the USS *Alabama* is probably the result of the friendly fire incident. Footsteps have been heard throughout the ship, especially the sleeping quarters. Visitors have also heard strange popping or tapping sounds in the bulkheads. Some people have even suddenly been overcome with sadness while walking through the ship. At least two full-bodied apparitions have made an appearance on the USS *Alabama*: the ghost of a cook seen preparing meals in the mess hall and the spirit of a blond sailor spotted in the sleeping quarters. This particular spirit seems to be a bit of a prankster. Some people think that he once snatched a woman's earring from her ear while she was walking through the sleeping quarters!

Mrs. Gilmer's Ghost
(Bay Minette, Alabama)

Did you know that libraries are some of the most haunted places in the United States? Could it be that libraries are spooky places, with their long stacks of books and dark, low-lit corners? Or could it be that librarians, by their very nature, are very dedicated souls who tend to stay on the job even after death? This is a good description of the ghost haunting the Bay Minette Public Library.

T.W. "Anne" Gilbert was the first librarian of the Bay Minette Public Library. When she started working in 1922, the library was housed in a rented room on Courthouse Square. In 1930, the city council gave the library a permanent home in a one-story Colonial building on land donated by Hampton D. Ewing. With financial assistance from the Works Progress Administration (WPA), Mrs. Gilmer was able to keep the library open during the Great Depression. On October 4,

1943, she was replaced by Pearlie Overstreet. Mrs. Gilmer may be gone, but librarians still feel her presence in the Bay Minette Public Library.

In the early 1990s, the director of the library, Charlotte Jones Cabiness Robertson, was walking through the stacks when she saw a book slowly inch itself off the shelf and fall to the floor. When she picked up the book, she noticed that it had been put in the wrong place. As she continued walking down the stacks, she found several other books on the floor that had been misplaced. As she picked them up, she began to take the ghost stories she had heard about the library more seriously.

Charlotte's suspicions that the library might really be haunted were confirmed one day when one of the workers moved Mrs. Gilmer's portrait back to its original place behind the

main desk. He told Charlotte that as soon as he hung up the portrait, he smelled the sweet scent of roses. Charlotte said that she and the other workers always smelled roses when something good had happened, such as an increase in the library's budget.

As time passed, the Bay Minette Public Library eventually outgrew the old building. As Charlotte was packing up the books, she told Mrs. Gilmer's ghost that she was welcome to move to the new library if she wished. A few days after the new library opened, Charlotte was in her office late one evening when the elevator rose up to the second floor. The door opened, but nobody stepped out. A few seconds later, the door closed, and the elevator returned to the first floor. Charlotte asked an electrician to examine the elevator, but he could find nothing wrong with it. Perhaps this was Mrs. Gilmer's way of announcing, "I'm back!"

Arkansas

HAUNTED HARDING UNIVERSITY
(SEARCY, ARKANSAS)

Galloway Women's College was dedicated in honor of Bishop Charles Betts Galloway in April 1889 by the Methodist Church. Women did not have many career opportunities at the time, and the college curriculum included studies in "homemaking" and "secretarial training." The school closed in June 1933 because of financial difficulties. In 1934, Harding College (now Harding University) took over the property. If the students are to be believed, Harding University may have gotten a ghost as a bonus when it bought the old school.

Harding University's ghost stories date back to the early 1920s, when the students attending Galloway Women's College who lived at Godden Hall, the dormitory, began to experience strange occurrences. Dorms are supposed to be a "home away from home," but Godden Hall looked more like something out of a nightmare, with arched doorways and Gothic towers with pointed, needle-like spires. One night, a student named Gertrude had just returned from a fancy party. She said goodnight to her boyfriend at the dorm entrance and went inside. Even though no one else was awake, she felt a little strange wearing her white evening gown, which made an annoying rustling sound with every step she took. Gertrude was walking down the hallway to her room when she heard a weird noise near the elevator. Her curiosity aroused, she walked over to investigate.

A few minutes later, the girls on Gertrude's floor were awakened by a piercing scream. The dorm mother heard the scream, too. She threw on her robe and rushed over to the scene of the commotion. When she got there, the door to the elevator was standing wide open. The dorm mother peered inside, expecting the worst. She was right. There, at the bottom of the elevator shaft, was the broken body of Gertrude. The police were called, and when they arrived, one of the girls told them that when she heard the blood-curdling scream, she threw open the door to her room just in time to catch a glimpse of a dark figure dashing down the hall, away from the elevator. Despite the suspicious circumstances of her demise, the police ruled Gertrude's death an accident.

Sometimes, ghosts become "restless spirits" when justice is not served. This, apparently, is the reason why Gertrude's ghost has returned to Harding University. For decades, students reported seeing the ghost of a pretty girl in a white dress floating—not walking—across campus. The November 4, 1950, issue of the school newspaper, the *Bison*, published a story about a girl who was sleeping in her room in Godden Hall when she woke up to get a drink of water. She stepped out into the hallway and walked past the now partially boarded-up elevator. She decided to peek inside the elevator through the crack between the boards. She was shocked to see a pretty blonde girl in a white dress standing inside the elevator. She forgot all about how thirsty she was and ran back to her

room screaming. She grabbed her roommate by the shoulders and shook her violently, saying, "You gotta go to the elevator and look inside!" Rubbing the sleep from her eyes, the girl replied in a groggy voice, "Okay." She stumbled out of the room and into the hallway. When her roommate didn't return as quickly as the girl thought she would, she slowly walked out of the room. As she neared the elevator, she was horrified by what she saw. There was her roommate, slouched against the wall, with a blank look on her face. In a low voice, she was mumbling the same sentence, over and over again: "She walked out of the elevator and right through the wall."

In 1951, Godden Hall was torn down. To save money, Harding University decided to use the bricks to build the Pattie Cobb Women's Residence Hall and the Claude Rogers Lee Music Center. Unfortunately, they found out that recycling materials from a haunted building is not a good idea because of the psychic residue that clings to them sometimes. The Pattie Cobb Women's Residence Hall seems to be ghost free, but a considerable amount of paranormal activity has been reported inside the Claude Rogers Lee Music Center. Students and instructors alike have heard phantom footsteps and the faint strains of piano music. Many people claim that the spectral figure of a woman looking down at them from an upper window in the music center is the spirit of Gertrude. Could it be that Gertrude's ghost haunts the music center? Possibly. It could be, though, that Gertrude has just had enough of dormitories.

The Mad Ghost of the Mayberry Inn (Hot Springs, Arkansas)

Sometimes, a traumatic event can bring on mental illness. Health professionals usually point to a combination of biological, psychological, and environmental factors when making an assessment about the state of a person's mind.

The trauma of war has caused thousands of soldiers to suffer from post-traumatic stress disorder, or PTSD for short. This may be what happened to David Mayberry.

Mayberry moved his family from Tennessee to Garland County, Arkansas, in 1832. They lived in a log cabin while he built a much larger house that he intended to turn into an inn. On the lower floor, one room was for men and the other for women. Inside each room was a tub filled with spring water. Mayberry believed that the curative powers of the spring water in the area would attract people to his inn.

The Mayberry Inn thrived in the 1850s. It became a popular stopping-off point between Hot Springs and Mount Ida. Prospectors eager to cash in on the region's large deposits of minerals stayed there, as well. Between 1861 and 1865, David took a break from innkeeping to fight in the American Civil War. By time the war had ended, he had been wounded sixteen times. Locals believe that blood poisoning from his wounds may have been responsible for his erratic behavior when he returned home. People claim that at night, he buried his gold, dug it back up, and then reburied it multiple times over the remainder of his life to prevent thieves from stealing it. After David died in 1880, a lawyer named Elias William Rector bought the inn, which he used as a summer home. His descendants still own the former Mayberry Inn to this day.

People living in and around Hot Springs have been telling ghost stories about the Mayberry Inn for generations. They said that a gang of outlaws who spent the night at the inn robbed and murdered several of the guests, most of whom had struck it rich in the mines.

People who swore they had no money were killed anyway. After the bandits left, David Mayberry set about cleaning up the mess. The bloodstains in one of the rooms seemed to resist all efforts to remove it. In frustration, David simply painted the floor brown.

The other ghost stories focus on David Mayberry's alleged insanity. In one of the ghost stories, he stabbed his wife in fit of anger and buried her in the fireplace. Many guests complained of hearing her cries coming from the fireplace at midnight. Another story has it that he drowned his infant son in the basement right after murdering his wife. For many years, people claimed to have heard the cries of a baby coming from an old bathtub in the basement. Keep in mind that these are legends, which means that the residents of Hot Springs might have come up with these tales to explain the strange sounds coming from the old inn as well as the weird behavior of the owner of the inn.

Florida

THE HAUNTED HOSPITAL
(PENSACOLA, FLORIDA)

A hospital is not the kind of place we'd like to spend a lot of our time, right?

Old hospitals, though, built in the architectural style of long ago, are a hot spot for spooky activity, especially if they are abandoned or now being used for some other purpose. As we pass through the dark hallways and peer into the rooms, we have the nagging feeling that someone who died or worked there years ago might still be around.

The Sacred Heart Hospital in Pensacola, Florida, is a good example of one of these old hospitals. It was built in the Gothic style. This means that the top of the building resembles a castle with wooden doors and a low wall running along the top of the building. When it opened in 1915, it was considered to be a state-of-the-art facility. In fact, it had the first bacterial, radiological, and therapeutic wards in the entire state.

For many years, patients and otall members believed that the Sacred Heart Hospital was haunted by the ghost of a nun. Unlike the ghosts in stories and movies that seem to delight in sneaking up on people and scaring them, this ghost was a kindly spirit. Some have reported feeling an invisible hand tapping them on the back of their shoulders. Apparently, she is one of those dedicated souls who is still on job long after she had passed on.

When a new hospital was built in 1965, the Sacred Heart Hospital was no longer used. The building became a liberal arts school until 1978. Then in 1980, the building was purchased by a group of investors called Tower East. The new owners cleaned up and restored the old building, using historic photographs as a guide. By the time the work was completed, the building looked much like it did when it first opened as a hospital.

Today, the structure is used as an office building. It also houses a number of small businesses on the lower floors, including a yoga studio, a veterinary clinic, and several restaurants. To this day, people talk about the mysterious figure that strolls down the halls and appears in doorways, usually for just a few seconds. The owners seem to have done such a good job restoring the building to its former appearance that the ghostly nun feels right at home there, even though it is no longer a hospital.

THE PERMANENT GUESTS OF THE KENWOOD INN
(ST. AUGUSTINE, FLORIDA)

The Kenwood Inn was a private residence before opening as an inn in 1865. The building continued to operate as an inn under a variety of different names through the modern era. The current owners, Pat and Ted Dubosz, say that reports of paranormal activity inside the inn began in the early 2000s, when Mark and Karianne Constant owned it.

Guests have reported being visited by ghosts in several of the rooms. A lady who was sleeping in Room 8 said that she was awakened during the night when a cat jumped on her bed. The startled woman sat up in bed and screamed when the cat disappeared. Room 17 on the third floor is said to be haunted, as well. A guest told the owners that she was on her way out the door when she happened to look back inside the room. She was shocked to see an elderly lady sitting in a chair. She was wearing a dress from the late nineteenth century, and her gray hair was tied back in a tight bun.

Room 7 is the most haunted room in the Kenwood Inn.

One night, a pair of sisters booked a night in the room. After they went to bed, one of the women was awakened by the sound of someone flipping the pages of a book. The next morning, she asked her sister if she had been reading during the night. Her sister replied that she had slept soundly all night long. Another guest said that someone pulled a comforter over her during the night.

Some experts in the paranormal believe the ghost might be the spirit of Raymond Laborde, who operated the inn in the 1880s. One of the

guests in the early 2000s told Mark Constant that she wanted Room 7 because she wanted to see the ghost of Raymond Laborde. She spent most of the day visiting the shops, restaurants, and historic sites of St. Augustine. When she returned to her room, she was unable to unlock the door, even though she had a key. The sheepish innkeeper explained to her that Mr. Laborde must have locked her out of the room.

Columbus, Georgia

Georgia

THE GHOST OF THE SPRINGER OPERA HOUSE (COLUMBUS, GEORGIA)

There are lots of haunted theaters in the South. Most of them are haunted by the ghosts of crew members or actors who died there. For example, shortly after the Wells Theater opened in Norfolk, Virginia, in 1913, a stagehand became entangled in one of the ropes as he fell from the catwalk and accidentally hanged himself. One evening in the late nineteenth century, an actress was sitting on the catwalk with a stagehand at the Petit Theater in New Orleans. They were watching a play when, suddenly, she fell off, crashing to her death. No one knows for sure if she jumped or if someone pushed her off, but these ghosts haunt the theater where they worked, some say, because they still feel like they have duties to perform. The ghost that haunts the Springer Opera House, on the other hand, still remains for an entirely different reason.

The Springer Opera House was designed by Frances Springer, an emigrant from Alsace, France, who believed that Georgia deserved a theater as grand as the ones in Europe. The theater opened its doors on February 21, 1871. A number of historic figures have appeared there over the years, including Franklin D. Roosevelt and American composer John Philip Sousa. However, the best-known actor at the Springer Opera House was Edwin Booth, the brother of John Wilkes Booth. Even though Edwin was a Unionist who openly disapproved of his brother's Southern sympathies, many Americans hated him anyway, simply because he was a close relative of the man who assassinated President Abraham Lincoln on April 14, 1865, in Ford's Theater. Immediately following the death of the president, Edwin and his actor father, Junius Booth, went into seclusion for many months. Edwin didn't return to the stage until January 1866, when he played the title role in *Hamlet* at the Winter Garden.

Edwin continued to perform in theaters across the United States, but his heart didn't seem to be in it anymore. Perhaps he suspected that people only came to see him because of his connection to the most hated man in America and not because they enjoyed his acting. However, when Edwin appeared in his celebrated role as Hamlet at the Springer Theater in 1876, his career received the jolt that it so sorely needed. The audience loved him and treated

him as one of America's greatest actors (which he was!). They probably realized that we can't choose the people we are related to. According to legend, Edwin announced to the audience at the Springer Opera House he was so appreciative of the warm reception they gave him that he vowed to return to the theater after his death. It would seem that Edwin kept his promise.

Stagehands tend to blame the ghost of Edwin Booth when props malfunction or when the doors open in small balconies that are no longer used. One evening, several patrons were standing in front of the portrait of Edwin Booth when one of three wine bottles on the bar suddenly tipped over, spilling wine all over the floor. Ghost hunters call this type of mischievous ghostly behavior "poltergeist activity." But it's not hard to believe this might be Edwin Booth's way of saying, "Hey, I'm still here, and I'm going to remain in the Springer Opera House forever because I love it!"

FORT PULASKI'S AMERICAN CIVIL WAR GHOSTS
(COCKSPUR ISLAND, GEORGIA)

Some of the most haunted places in the South are the brick-and-mortar American Civil War–era forts that guard the coastline. One of these forts, Fort Pulaski, was built between 1843 and 1847 on Cockspur Island off the coast of Georgia. Over 25 million bricks went into the fort's construction. In 1861, Confederate forces easily wrestled Fort Pulaski away from the 134 Union troops who were occupying it at the time. However, a year later, the bombardment of the fort by the Union army resulted in the surrender of Colonel Charles H. Olmstead's Confederate troops. In 1864, Fort Pulaski was turned into a makeshift prison for 550 Confederate captives. Their diet consisted of rats, dogs, cats, and anything else they could catch. Thirteen Confederate soldiers died in the prison, mostly because of its inhumane living conditions. Fort Pulaski was decommissioned in

1880. The fort stood abandoned for many years before being turned over to the Department of the Interior in 1933.

Fort Pulaski's reputation as a haunted fort began not long after. Visitors have reported hearing footsteps walking in the grassy areas outside of the fort. A few people claim to have heard ghostly voices calling their names. It's not unusual at all for people to report an invisible presence standing next to them or walking beside them. Visitors have seen the full-bodied apparitions of Union and Confederate soldiers standing guard both inside and outside.

One of the most active parts of the fort is the stairway where a man who was killed in the 1862 bombardment was carried down to the basement. People standing in Colonel Olmstead's room have become overwhelmed by a feeling of depression—probably the same sadness that he must have felt when he was forced to surrender Fort Pulaski to the Union forces.

The most publicized paranormal occurrence at Fort Pulaski occurred during the filming of the American Civil War movie *Glory* in the late 1980s. A large number of Civil War reenactors were used in the movie's battle scenes. A group of "soldiers" was walking through the parade grounds when they were approached by a young man wearing a Confederate lieutenant's uniform. In an angry voice, he scolded the men for not saluting him when they passed by. He ordered them to fall into formation and turn around. When they did as they were told, the irate officer was gone. At that moment, history became a little too real for the reenactors.

CHAPTER 5

Kentucky

THE WITCH'S GHOST
(CAMPBELLSVILLE, KENTUCKY)

Southern folklore includes many legends about witches. Many of these women used herbs as medicine and treated people in areas where there were no trained physicians. Most of the legends about witches focus on people who are foolish enough to anger these women. But this story is much different than any of the typical, run-of-the-mill Southern ghost stories. This matter involves a supposed curse and the Spurlington Train Tunnel.

Work on the tunnel began in 1867. Digging out the 1,900-foot-long tunnel was difficult, because workers had to bore through limestone. Today, the Spurlington Tunnel is avoided by many locals because of the legend of Nancy Bass. She was a homeless woman who slept in barns and haystacks. With her wild hair and broken teeth, she probably looked like the typical witch. Many people believed that she was a witch because of her habit cursing farmers who tried to chase her off their property. Some people were so afraid of her that they talked about tying her to a stake and burning her.

Aunt Nancy, as people called her, seemed to enjoy her reputation as a witch. Legend has it that one day, she told a crowd of people who were threatening to burn her that she could only be killed by a silver bullet. Then, one night, her lifeless body was found on a farm owned by a man named Wright. Locals were not surprised at all when the coroner found a silver bullet buried in her heart. To this day, her ghost has never left the area.

But she is believed to haunt the Spurlington Tunnel because of a different theory about her death. Some locals say that Jesse James and his gang shot and killed her because she saw them trying to hide their gold inside of the tunnel. Rumor has it James and company buried Nancy Bass along with the loot they had stolen before their leaving town. So far, no one has discovered any buried treasure—or the corpse of Nancy Bass. Yet a number of people claim to have photographed her ghost at the entrance of the abandoned tunnel. But is her ghost lingering because she's guarding treasure or because this is the home of her earthly remains?

THE ANGRY GHOST OF OCTAGON HALL (FRANKLIN, KENTUCKY)

Andrew Jackson Caldwell felt very close to Octagon Hall, probably because it took him twelve years to build it. By the time he finished the house, it had become a labor of love for him. Yet the happiness he felt ended on February 13, 1862, when a company of Confederate soldiers camped out on his lawn to find food and rest. They departed just before the Union army arrived at Octagon Hall. Suspecting that Caldwell had fed the Confederate soldiers and treated the injured men, the commanding Union officer decided to cause trouble. He killed all of the cattle and dumped one of the cows in the well, poisoning the water. When he threatened to kill Caldwell too, the angry old man replied, "Go ahead! My brother just left, and when he comes back, he'll kill you too!" Fearing Caldwell's wrath, the Union officer ordered his men to leave the plantation.

Andrew Jackson Caldwell's descendants continued living in Octagon Hall until 1918, when Dr. Miles Williams bought the house. After he died in 1954, the mansion was converted into rental property. In 2001, the Octagon Hall

Foundation acquired the property and opened it up to the public. Tour guides at Octagon Hall believe the ghost of Andrew Jackson Caldwell is responsible for most of the weird things that go on there. They say that he's the ghost that has been seen from a distance driving a wagon across the property.

A group of American Civil War reenactors may also have made the acquaintance of the original owner of Octagon Hall. Several of the men decided to prove their bravery by spending the night in the house. They soon regretted their decision when the sounds of footsteps and the opening and closing of doors kept them awake all night long. The next morning, the sleepy men went into one of the bedrooms and were surprised the find the outline of a body on the mattress. Shivers ran up their spines when it occurred to them that they were not alone in Octagon Hall during the night.

Louisiana

AMERICA'S MOST HAUNTED HOUSE (ST. FRANCISVILLE, LOUISIANA)

Did you know that you can visit what the Smithsonian Institute calls "the Most Haunted House in America?" Well, not only can you go there, but you can spend the night there, at the Myrtles Plantation bed-and-breakfast. The house is so haunted that the employees give tours of the house—at night, of course.

The Myrtles was built as several sections over many years. The earliest part was built in 1794 by General David Bradford, who fled to Louisiana during the Whiskey Rebellion to avoid capture by President Washington. He lived there alone for two years while the main part of the house was being built. His daughter Sarah Matilda inherited the house after her parents' death and lived there with her husband, Judge Clark Woodruff. Even though he was a judge, Woodruff was rumored to have been involved in some shady business dealings. One evening, the judge was meeting with several of his business cronies in the gentleman's Parlor when he sensed that someone was listening. He got up from the sofa and threw open the pocket doors. Just outside the door was a house servant named Chloe, who had been listing to the judge's conversation. In a fit of rage, he dragged the girl to the kitchen and cut off her left ear. Plastic surgery was not practiced in Louisiana at this time, so Chloe began wearing a green turban so that people would not know that she had only one ear.

For several weeks afterward, Chloe's greatest fear was that the judge would force her to work in the cotton fields because he did not feel like he could trust her anymore. When the birthday of one of his daughters arrived, Chloe concocted a scheme to make the judge eternally grateful to her. While she was mixing the dough for the girl's birthday cake, Chloe decided to add just enough oleander to make the girls sick. Oleander is an extremely poisonous plant that grows in Louisiana. Chloe had planned to offer to nurse the girls back to health and get back into the family's good graces. Chloe added too much oleander to the dough, and as a result, two of the girls died. Their father was so irate that he ordered her to be hanged from one of the live oak trees on the plantation. Because she had committed such a terrible crime, her body was thrown into the Mississippi River instead of being given a Christian burial.

The ghosts of the two little girls are still hanging around the old plantation house. Guests who took one of the Myrtles' ghost tours have said that they were standing in the parlor where the girls had their last meal when they felt someone tugging on their pants or skirt. Women have also felt a small, cold hand grab their hand. When this writer was on one these nightly tours, the tour guide had just talked about the ghosts of the little girls when a woman screamed that someone was pulling on her skirt. With a grin on his face, her husband admitted that he had grabbed her dress. Everyone laughed except for the joker's wife.

People say that the spirit of poor Chloe also makes an occasional appearance at the only home she had ever known. People who have spent the night at the Myrtles have felt someone pull the blankets up to their neck or down to their feet. However, when they turn on the light, they are the only ones in the room. In 1978, a photograph inadvertently captured the image of a black woman in an old cotton dress and an apron standing in the space between the main house and the gift shop. She was clearly wearing a turban. Seeing is believing, right?

The next owners of the house were the Ruffin Gray Sterling family from Scotland. The couple had eight boys and one girl. Seven of the boys died in the Civil War; the last remaining son was shot and killed in the dining room of the Myrtles in 1866. Not surprisingly, Mrs. Sterling mourned for her dead children for the rest of her life. Evidence suggests that her ghost is still strongly attached to the French Room on the first floor. From this room, which was Mrs. Sterling's day room, she issued orders to the servants and wrote letters. One Halloween in the early 2000s, a high school actress who was going to enact the role of Chloe during a play at the house was in the French Room, all by herself. At the time, the room was completely dark. She entered the bathroom and applied her makeup. She then lit a candle and walked back into the room. She was practicing her role when, all at once, a blue mist appeared in a corner of the room. Within a few seconds, the mist morphed into the form of a woman. The girl walked toward the apparition to get a look at her face, but her candle went out. Terrified, the poor girl dropped her candle and took a few quick steps to the bathroom. Just before she reached the door, it slammed shut in her face. Too scared to move, she lay down on the floor and screamed until the tour guide on the other side of her house came to her rescue. The first thing she said to him when he entered the

room was "Couldn't you have run any faster?" Actually, it only took the guy two and a half minutes, but it seemed much longer to her. Oh, she also vowed never to return to the Myrtles ever again—and she didn't!

Mrs. Sterling's daughter Sarah also experienced tragedy inside the Myrtles. She married a lawyer named William Winter. She and her husband had three lovely children. However, following the Civil War, the couple's happiness came to an abrupt end. In 1867, one of their daughters died of yellow fever. Two months later, in January 1868, their other daughter, Katie, contracted the disease, and the doctors were unable to help her. Sarah, who was at her wits' end, sent for a voodoo queen named Cleo from a neighboring plantation. Cleo spent all night with the girl in what is now the William Winter Room, chanting and performing rituals. As the sun came up the next day, Cleo announced to the family that Katie would recover. Unfortunately, the girl died within a few hours. Enraged, William had Cleo lynched from a tree in the plantation. Sometimes people pin the blame on someone else when there seems to be no apparent justification for their suffering, and this is what happened to poor Cleo. She did her best, but her best wasn't good enough. Her restless spirit has been sighted walking around the plantation and peering down at guests who are trying to sleep in the William Winter Room.

You would think that Sarah Winter had had enough misery in her life, but fate had something else in store for the poor woman. One day in 1871, William Winter was tutoring his son when a man rode up to the house on horseback, yelling that he needed a lawyer. Winter walked over to the front door and opened it. Immediately, he was struck by a bullet in the chest. He staggered over to the staircase and attempted to make his way up to his wife's bedroom. His strength gave out, though, and he collapsed and died on the seventeenth step. Heartbroken, Sarah spent the rest of her life in her bedroom. Eventually, she lost the will to live and starved herself to death. Visitors to her bedroom claim to have heard the sound of someone sobbing in a corner of the room. People standing in the room have also heard someone trudging up the stairs and falling down on the seventeenth step. Like many ghosts, William Winter seems doomed to re-enact his death for eternity.

Would you like to sleep in the same bed with a ghost? Well, you can in the John W. Leake Room in the Myrtles. During the Civil War, a Confederate officer was brought to the main house for treatment of a bullet wound in his left leg. The doctor and their servants did their best to help, but within a couple of days, gangrene set in, and the man's leg was amputated. Some guests claim to have awakened during the night with shooting pains in their left leg. Other people say that they woke up when someone blew smoke in their face. It turns out that John Leake, one of the owners of the house, smoked cigars. Could this have been his way of telling the guests, "Get out of my bed!"

In the foyer of the Myrtles, one can gaze into one of the most haunted mirrors in the United States. In the 1800s, when someone died at home, the mourners draped sheets or blankets over all of the mirrors in the house so that the person's spirit would not become accidentally trapped in the glass forever. Legend has it that if a visitor stares into the floor-length mirror, long dead faces will suddenly appear. Also, what appear to be child-like fingerprints can be seen along the left side of the mirror. Some people think that the spirits of Sarah and her two daughters are trapped here. Few residents, it seems, ever really leave the Myrtles after death.

St. Louis Cemetery No. 1 (New Orleans, Louisiana)

Everything about New Orleans is unique. The authentic Cajun cuisine draws thousands of tourists to the city's fine restaurants every year. The eighteenth- and nineteenth-century architecture of the French Quarter reflects the influence of its early Spanish and French residents. Music lovers come here for the live Dixieland music that resounds from the bars and cafés. The culture of the city definitely has a distinctive New Orleans feel. However, some say that New Orleans's most peculiar feature is St. Louis Cemetery No. 1.

St. Louis Cemetery No. 1 is the oldest cemetery in New Orleans. It was founded in 1789 at the corner of St. Louis Street and Basin Street. The cemetery is best known for its aboveground burials. Most of the dead are buried in vaults and mausoleums because New Orleans is below sea level. This means that coffins buried underground would eventually be washed out when it rains and the water level rises. The deceased are laid out in wooden coffins inside the tomb for one year. During this time, the tomb becomes so hot that the remains decompose very quickly. This is the reason why these tombs are called "ovens." Once a year has passed, the remains are placed in a bag at the rear of the tomb. This strange arrangement creates room for the next family member who passes away.

Not surprisingly, an old cemetery in a city with this much history is bound to produce a number of ghost stories. One of these legends is about a man named Henry Vignes. Witnesses describe him as a tall, sad-looking man wearing a white shirt. People say that this man taps them on their shoulder and asks them to help him find his tomb. He then turns, begins walking, and slowly fades away. He is clearly a "lost soul" who, some say, is caught between this world and the next.

The most famous "permanent resident" of St. Louis Cemetery No. 1 is undoubtedly Marie Laveau (1801–1881), the Voodoo Queen of New Orleans. She was also revered in her lifetime as an herbalist healer. Her tomb is pretty easy to find because it is covered with Xs visitors have scratched on the side for good luck. They have also left offerings, such as flowers, money, bones, candles, and jewelry, in the hope that she will grant their wishes. Visitors who have encountered her ghost describe her as being "unhappy," to say the least. People have seen her walking around her tomb at night, muttering curses under her breath. One day, a man who was standing in front of her tomb was slapped by an invisible hand. Other visitors claim to have felt icy fingers touching their neck and hands when they were standing near her tomb. Some tourists swear that they saw a group of nude phantoms performing Voodoo rituals at her tomb. Marie Laveau is still one of New Orleans's biggest draws, even though she had been dead for over 140 years!

Deer Island

CHAPTER 7

Mississippi

DEER ISLAND
(BILOXI, MISSISSIPPI)

Deer Island lies along the Gulf of Mexico, not too far offshore from Biloxi. It is not what you would call a vacation hotspot or a tropical paradise— unless you are a bird or reptile. But this 647-acre piece of floating real estate is a Mississippi Coastal Preserve area. This means the only living inhabitants are deer, turtles, and multiple bird species. The tale fishermen tell of the headless ghost of Deer Island has been sending shivers up the spines of locals, children, and tourists for almost one hundred years.

In the eighteenth century, a pirate captain anchored his ship just off the beach of Deer Island. He ordered his crew to unload a large chest of gold that they had stolen from several merchant ships. The captain was a very superstitious man. He told his men to dig a large, deep hole in the middle of the island and place the chest of gold inside of it. After his men had carried out his orders, the captain asked if anyone would be willing to stand guard over the treasure. The only one who volunteered was a young man who had just recently joined the band of pirates. With a broad smile on his face, the captain asked the young pirate to come forward.

When the young man was just a few feet away, the captain raised a sword that he had been hiding behind his back and lopped off the pirate's head with a single stroke. Blood was still gushing from the man's headless corpse when the captain ordered his crew to dump it into the hole. The men threw the head into the brush. But while his men were burying their unfortunate comrade, the captain explained their friend's headless ghost would watch over the buried treasure for eternity. For over two centuries, people living in Biloxi told this story to each other, but few really believed it. Their disbelief vanished almost overnight after three fishermen had a ghostly encounter on Deer Island in the 1920s.

Exhausted from the day's fishing, the men anchored their little boat offshore and decided to camp out on the island for the night. They cooked some of their catch over a campfire and lay down on their blankets for a well-deserved rest on what they assumed was a deserted islanded. Around midnight, one of the men heard something crashing through the palmetto fronds. Then, against the moonlight, he saw a headless skeleton staggering toward them. In a quivering voice, he yelled, "Wake up! Run to the boat!"

The terrified fishermen spent the rest of the night on the boat. The next morning, they returned to Deer Island to pick up their blankets and cooking utensils. All of their gear was right where they had left it, but their midnight intruder had vanished. The men had a story to tell their friends and relatives when they returned to Biloxi, but no one knows for sure if the headless ghost was actually guarding the treasure or looking for his lost head. What do you think?

ROCK AND ROLL CEMETERY
(OCEAN SPRINGS, MISSISSIPPI)

Some of the oldest cemeteries in the United States are family cemeteries. Many of these cemeteries have been abandoned or are no longer in use because the family members have passed on or moved away. No one knows for certain how the Rock and Roll Cemetery acquired its name, though older residents recall that teenagers would drive out to the cemetery in the 1950s to play rock and roll music. Decades later, teenagers continue to flock there to have fun and scare each other by telling ghost stories.

In 1902, then-owner of the property Mrs. M.V. Russell sold one acre of her land to use as a family cemetery. Surrounded by woods, young people now recall urban legends in the dark, telling stories that folklorists say focus on strange or supernatural events and are gruesome in nature. Most of these tales are set in modern times and are really just exaggerations of actual occurrences.

One urban legend surrounding the Rock and Roll Cemetery involves an old lady who is said to sit in a rocking chair over one of the graves. When anyone walks or drives past her, she shakes her fist and yells. She has even been known to chase people out of the graveyard! However, this story might have been inspired by an old rocking chair that was once found in the woods.

Some people say the road to the cemetery has fourteen curves leading in but only thirteen curves leading out. Strange sounds like cries, screams, and moans have been reported inside. And teenagers claim there is an eerie glow on the limb of a tree from which a man hanged himself.

None of these stories have any basis in fact, we remind you. Several years ago, Chicago

Paranormal Investigators spent the night in the cemetery and recorded no evidence of paranormal activity. Of course, anyone who visits should keep in mind the cemetery is a sacred place and should be treated with the greatest respect.

CHAPTER 8

North Carolina

THE FLYING SPIRITS OF CHIMNEY ROCK
(RUTHERFORD, NORTH CAROLINA)

Many legends have sprung up around geological oddities. Most of these natural sites and landmarks are caves or mountains. And for generations, the citizens of Rutherford, North Carolina, have been telling tales about a three hundred-foot-tall rock tower called Chimney Rock. It stands above Hickory Nut Gorge, and many tourists go there for its spectacular view of Lake Lure. However, some curiosity-seekers make the trip to Chimney Rock in the hope of seeing its airborne spirits.

The first account of the flying ghosts of Chimney Rock was reported on July 31, 1806. An eight-year-old girl named Elizabeth Reeves and her older brother Morgan were playing in the woods around Chimney Rock when they saw something in the sky that haunted their dreams for the rest of their lives. Soaring above and around were thousands of human-like figures in white gowns. Terrified, the children called to their mother, Patsy Reeves, and their sister Polly. Soon, they were also joined by four of their neighbors. For almost an hour, they watched swarms of white-clad people flying to the top of Chimney Rock! The spectacle ended when three of the figures led the rest of the flying beings into the sky, where they vanished from sight. A few weeks later, the story of their unbelievable sighting was published in the *Raleigh Register and Gazette*.

A different sort of heavenly display took occurred at Chimney Rock in 1811, as a much larger crowd of people gasped at the sight of two armies fighting each other in the clouds above the rocky monolith.

They claimed to have heard the screams of dying men and horses and the clanging sound of swords clashing against each other. This story was so sensational that it was run in newspapers across the entire United States, and for over two hundred years, the people of Rutherford have awaiting the return of the flying ghosts of Chimney Rock.

THE WEALTHY SPIRITS OF THE BILTMORE ESTATE (ASHEVILLE, NORTH CAROLINA)

Around the turn of the nineteenth century, the Vanderbilts were one of the richest families in the United States. They made their fortune primarily in railroad and steamboats. In 1886,

George Washington Vanderbilt II constructed a 250-room mansion in Asheville, North Carolina. It is the largest privately owned home in the country. After George died of an appendicitis in 1914, his wife, Edith, inherited the estate. Because the upkeep of the property was so costly, Edith soon found herself low on funds. In 1930, she had to open up her magnificent mansion for public tours. Thousands of people have visited the Biltmore Estates over the years, including Jackie Kennedy and Theodore Roosevelt. Most come to sample the lavish lifestyle of the rich and famous Vanderbilt family. However, guests also travel to the Biltmore to check out its ghosts.

Strange sounds are said to echo through the rooms and hallways of the mansion. Employees working late at night have heard parties going on in the pool area though it was drained long ago. Guests passing through seemingly empty rooms have heard whispered conversations, as if they were eavesdropping on the ghosts.

George Vanderbilt's spirit seems to be an active presence in the mansion. Maybe he feels like it's still his house, even though he's dead. His ghost has been seen reading one of the hundreds of books in the mansion's library. (There are enough books in the room to keep him busy for many years to come!) And Vanderbilt might also be the playful ghost who trips employees as they walk through the Banquet Hall.

An employee named L.A. Steward has had a number of spooky encounters inside and outside of the Biltmore. One day, he was walking toward the gift shops, which had served as stables for Vanderbilt's horses years ago. Just as he walked inside, he saw half of a horse—the lower half—standing in the hallway. Maybe the ghost horse did not have enough energy to fully materialize. Though at that moment, Steward recalled the clopping of horses' hooves that he had been hearing for a long time.

Another strange experience happened in the basement hallway between the laundry and floral department. As he walked toward the floral room, he saw a mean-looking middle-aged woman walk inside. At that moment, he sensed he had made the acquaintance of Mrs. King, Vanderbilt's no-nonsense housekeeper. She was definitely not the type of ghost that you would want to bump into in the dark.

THE DEVIL'S TRAMPING GROUND (CHATHAM COUNTY, NORTH CAROLINA)

Many years ago, when people were faced with a natural phenomenon they could not understand, they often came up with a fantastic explanation. Such is the case with a barren circle forty feet wide in Chatham County, North Carolina. Settlers who discovered this strange patch of land in the mid-1700s claimed the devil himself created it centuries ago. Lost in thought, he wanders around in circles while trying to come up with strategies for snaring human souls. People thought that the ground must be cursed because no plants would grow there.

As time passed, the tales about the Devil's Tramping Ground grew. People said that if you threw an object inside the circle before nightfall, you would find it outside of the circle the next morning. Supposedly, several men who were brave—or foolish—enough to sleep inside the Devil's Tramping Ground were found dead the next morning. Dogs, it seems, are smarter than people because they refuse to venture inside the circle.

Of course, there are some rational explanations for the lifeless circle. Some locals suggest that it was made by horses or mules that walked around in circles while grinding grain. Scientists have pointed out, however, that places like these eventually become overgrown by grass. The simplest explanation, scientists say, is that nothing grows in the circle because the ground is sterile. Nevertheless, the mystery continues.

South Carolina

The Ghostly Actress of the Abbeville Opera House (Abbeville, South Carolina)

In the early 1900s, a group of concerned citizens campaigned for the construction of an opera house in Abbeville, South Carolina. Construction of the opera house was completed in 1908, and live performances were held there for about seven years until 1914, when it became a movie theater. Silent movies were shown there primarily until they were replaced by sound movies in the 1930s. The old opera house continued showing movies until the 1950s, when it closed its doors. In 1968, the Abbeville Opera House was restored, thanks in large part to the work of the Abbeville Community Theater group. Today, it looks much the same as it did when it opened in 1908.

The possibility that the old opera house might be haunted was suggested while restoration efforts were continuing. Strange things began happening for no apparent reason. Sometimes, the curtains would get stuck or the lights would go off and on by themselves. Eventually, the blame for the interruptions was place on the "ghost chair." Stage crew members discovered that whenever anyone moved or touched a particular chair, something would go wrong with the productions.

Some actors and crew members believe that the Abbeville Opera House is haunted by the ghost of an actress who died shortly after performing there. One night at the end of a play, one of the actors claimed to have seen a woman standing up in the balcony applauding. He recalled that she was wearing old-fashioned clothing and vanished after a few seconds. For months, ghostly clapping was heard in the balcony, even when there was no audience present.

THE LEAMINGTON LIGHTHOUSE (HILTON HEAD ISLAND, SOUTH CAROLINA)

Through most of the 1800s, the coastal areas of Southern states were dotted with lighthouses. Thousands of ships were able to find safe harbor on dark and stormy nights by following the lighthouses' powerful beacons, which guided them around the rocky shoals. It was the job of lighthouse keepers to make sure the light burned all night long. One of these dedicated lighthouse keepers is memorialized in the ghost legend of the Leamington Lighthouse.

It was built between 1879 and 1880 to guide ships into Port Royal Sound. In 1898, the worst nightmare of any lighthouse keeper—a hurricane—ravaged the South Carolina coast. Keeping the light burning in hurricane-force winds was a challenge, to say the least. Adam Fripp was fully aware that the lives of the crew of any ship unfortunate enough to be in Port Royal Sound that night were in his hands. He was running around, making sure everything was in working order, when he clutched his chest and collapsed. Fripp had a heart attack at the worst possible time. Luckily for him, his twenty-one-year-old daughter, Caroline, was able to help him to his feet and walk him out of the lighthouse to the keeper's house not far away. After she got her father in bed, he sat up, clasped Caroline's hand, and made her promise that she would keep the light burning. Just as he fell back in bed and gasped his last breath, Caroline assured him that she would do what he asked.

Caroline then put on her blue dress and her most comfortable shoes and ran around Hilton Head Island, telling residents to seek high ground. The courage of the dutiful daughter has inspired generations of children on Hilton Head Island. The lesson they learned from Caroline's example is that children should do what their parents ask them to do. Her fate following her heroic act is unknown. Some people say that she followed her father in death three weeks later. Others insist that she lived a long, happy life. What most people do agree on, though, is that the lady in blue still walks the grounds of the lighthouse in bad weather. The fact that the lighthouse was deactivated in 1932 doesn't seem to matter.

Tennessee

MAGNOLIA MANOR
(BOLIVAR, TENNESSEE)

Judge Austin Miller built Magnolia Manor in 1849. The Georgia Colonial mansion has twelve-inch-thick walls, fourteen-foot-ceilings, and double parlors. One day in 1862, Judge Miller had four unwelcome visitors—Union generals Logan, McPherson, Sherman, and Grant. The judge was loyal to the Confederacy, and his wife didn't want the Union men there either, but she grudgingly allowed them to use only half of the mansion.

At dinner that evening, General Sherman lived up to his reputation of being a surly man by making rude remarks about the people of the South, prompting Mrs. Miller to throw down her napkin and rush out of the dining room with tears in her eyes. General Grant, who had not attended the dinner, caught up with Mrs. Miller at the back porch and asked her what was wrong. In a quivering voice, she told the general about Sherman's comments. Grant left the porch and stormed into the dining room. He angrily ordered Sherman to apologize to the lady of the house. Sherman obeyed the order from his superior officer and marched out of the room. As he stormed past the main staircase, he slashed the bannister with his sabre. The cut mark is a reminder that even generals don't like to be told that they have done something wrong.

In 1985, Elaine Cox bought the Millers' house and opened it up as a bed-and-breakfast. She soon realized that even when no guests were present, she never felt truly alone in the house. Weird things like doors opening and closing by themselves and a collection of dolls that moved on their own occurred on a regular basis. One room that really freaked out Elaine was the C.A. Miller Suite. One night, she was sleeping in the room when she was awakened by the creaking sound of the rocking chair. Elaine leaped out of bed. For just a few seconds, she caught a glimpse of a lady sitting in the chair before she just faded away. Elaine recalled the figure was wearing a dress dating back to the mid-1800s. Ghostly activity occurs in the 1849 Room, as well. Many guests have complained about having the blankets pulled off their beds in that room. A man was sleeping in the 1849 Room when he was startled by a female apparition pulling on the sleeve of his pajamas. He was so frightened that he ran out of the house, climbed into his car, and took off! The man didn't even take the time to grab his suitcase. Do you blame him?

So many weird things have happened in the 1849 Room that Elaine Cox invited a psychic from Natchez, Mississippi, named Jan Linley to try to communicate with the spirit in the room. Jan arrived late in the evening with several of her friends. The group entered the 1849 Room

and sat down in front of the fireplace. Hanging above the fireplace was the portrait of an eighteen-year-old girl named Priscilla, who died in the room. The investigation had just begun when suddenly, the portrait flew across the room! Elaine's first thought was that someone was playing a prank, so she checked Jan's hands and the hands of the other people in the room. She found no sign of trickery.

The brick cottage behind Maple Manor is also a very spooky place. Before the American Civil War, it was used as slave quarters and as a cookhouse. Not surprisingly, Adeline, the cook, is still here, probably because she considered the cookhouse to be her own private domain. However, the cookhouse is haunted by other creatures as well. Guests have heard a parrot squawking and talking inside the cottage. Even a ghost cat is said to prowl around the cookhouse. Elaine thinks that he is the ghost of a cat that belonged to one of the Millers' daughters, Annie.

After the cat died, the town wouldn't allow Annie to bury the cat in the town cemetery, so she buried him in the Miller family plot. She even gave him his own tombstone. Annie really loved her cat!

The Chapel Hill Light (Chapel Hill, Tennessee)

Do you know what ghost lights are? Well, ghost lights are orbs (balls of light) that people have seen flitting around spooky, out-of-the-way places at night. Some of the most common ghost lights are the ones people have seen while driving past cemeteries. Reports like these are easy prove untrue. In most cases, these ghostly orbs are just the reflection of the headlights bouncing off of polished surfaces like tombstones. However, some reports of ghost lights are more difficult to disprove, like the Chapel Hill Ghost Light.

Locals have reported sightings of the Chapel Hill Light at the railroad tracks for many years.

Descriptions of the strange light vary, depending on who is telling the story. Some witnesses describe it as a disk that hovers three or four feet above the ground and then blinks out. Other people say that the light is actually a cluster of three lights that appear on one side of the tracks. A resident of Chapel Hill named John Rickman said that when the light floats over the tracks, it sways back and forth. When curiosity-seekers follow the light, it vanishes and reappears behind them.

The residents of Chapel Hill have told several different versions of the backstory surrounding the Chapel Hill Light. The majority of the tales are set around the railroad tracks, involving railroad workers who met their grisly end during the late 1800s and early 1900s. In one version of the story, a brakeman was walking across the tops of the train cars, setting the brakes. All at once, the train lurched forward, knocking the brakeman off a train car. He fell on the tracks, right in the path of a passing train, which cut off his head.

According to a second version, a signalman standing by a derailed train waves a lantern as a warning to an oncoming train to slow down, but before the train engineer can reduce his speed, the train hits the signalman and decapitates him, too! Some say the signalman was actually an old man who was walking down the tracks with his lantern on a rainy night when he tripped on one of the railroad ties. It is said that he hit his head on one of the rails and was knocked unconscious. A few minutes later, a train roared by, cutting off the poor man's head. All of these variants, however, end with the ghost of a man walking down the tracks at night with his lantern as he searches for his lost head.

Not all of the Chapel Hill Light legends involve railroad workers, though. Residents also talk about a man who was standing on the railroad tracks one night, waving his lantern, so that the engineer would slow down and pick him up, just as he had done many times before. However, this time, the train had a new engineer who was not aware of the man's habit of signaling the train at night for a ride. By the time the new engineer saw the midnight rider, it was too late. The train hit the man and—you guessed it—cut off his head.

Of course, there is probably a rational explanation for the ghost light, isn't there? Scientists tell us that most of these mysterious balls of light are actually formed by methane gas, also known as "swamp gas." Methane is produced by rotting vegetation, and sometimes the gas ignites, forming these weird little balls of light.

The scientific explanation sounds pretty cool, but the ghost tales are much more fun, aren't they?

CHAPTER 11

Virginia

The Martha Washington Inn
(Abingdon, Virginia)

Historians estimate that 620,000 soldiers died in the American Civil War. In fact, more soldiers died in the war than in any other war the United States has fought. When you have a death toll this high, you are probably going to have a lot of ghost stories about that war, right? Well, a large number of Southern ghost stories are connected somehow to the Civil War. The pain and suffering that people endured at this time, both on and off the battlefield, has been preserved in hundreds of legends. However, a surprising percentage of these Civil War ghost legends are love stories.

Two of these romantic tales took place at a large mansion in Abingdon, Virginia. It was built by General Francis Preston in 1832 for $15,000. (This was a lot of money back then!) Because the mansion was so large, it was converted into a girls' school, Martha Washington College, in 1858. When the war broke out in 1861, a number of the students served as nurses. Until the end of the war in 1865, they treated the injuries of an untold number of Confederate soldiers who were brought here. In 1932, the school closed down, and then three years later, the mansion became the Martha Washington Inn.

The ghosts that haunt the inn aren't scary, just sad. Both of these tales date back to the American Civil War, naturally. In one of these legends, a young Confederate soldier was ordered to report on the movements of the Union army in the area. He was on his way to

General Robert E. Lee's headquarters to tell what he had learned when he decided to stop off at the Martha Washington Inn and say goodbye to his girlfriend. To keep from being seen by the Union army, he sneaked into the school through a cave running under the school and then through a hidden stairway. His girlfriend was delighted at the sight of her boyfriend, but their embrace was cut short when a pair of blue-clad soldiers barged into the room. Before the young Confederate could draw his pistol, the Union soldiers shoot him dead. Crying hysterically, the girl rushed to her boyfriend's side as his life's blood pooled around his motionless body.

For many years, employees at the college and at the inn have tried to scrub off the bloodstain. The staff used strong soap, sandpaper, and paint, but nothing worked. A day or so later, the dark patch of blood reappeared. One of the owners of the inn had the bright idea of simply placing carpeting over the bloodstain. A few days later, holes appeared in the carpet. Talk about a stubborn ghost stain!

Another ghost story set in the Martha Washington Inn is about a Union prisoner named John Stoves. The company of Confederate soldiers who had captured John brought him to the college for treatment of his wounds. He was taken to Room 217, where a student named Beth bandaged his wounds. Well, guess what happened! You're right—Beth fell in love with the handsome prisoner. It didn't matter that he was a Union soldier because, as we all know, love is blind.

Beth did her best to take care of John, but the young man grew weaker and weaker. She had told him she played the violin, so one night, John pleaded with her to play a song for him. Beth told him that she would be happy to play for him and went back to her room to get her violin.

She was tuning it when John took his last breath and passed away, and to this day, guests and employees at the Martha Washington Inn have reported hearing someone playing the violin late at night.

Perhaps nurse Beth still intends to play one last song for her love John, the Union soldier.

THE HISTORIC HAUNTS OF FORT MONROE (HAMPTON, VIRGINIA)

Construction of Fort Monroe was completed in 1834, and the fort was under the control of Union forces during the American Civil War. Several historical figures are connected with the fort. Edgar Allan Poe served as a sergeant at the fort from October 1828 until April 1829, and Abraham Lincoln inspected Fort Monroe during his visit on June 2, 1862. After the Civil War ended in 1865, the former president of the Confederacy, Jefferson Davis, was imprisoned at Fort Monroe. Following the Emancipation

Proclamation, over ten thousand freed slaves lived in the surrounding area. Fittingly, they referred to Fort Monroe as "Freedom Fort." After the fort was decommissioned on September 15, 2011, President Barack Obama designated portions of the fort as national monuments.

Fort Monroe has a reputation as being one of the best preserved masonry forts in the United States. If the folklore can be believed, the spirits of some of the people who lived and visited the fort are preserved at Fort Monroe, too. The ghosts of Abraham Lincoln and Edgar Allan Poe have been sighted inside the building, while Jefferson Davis's ghost prefers to walk around the fort in the evening.

Despite these celebrity apparitions, a host of less famous spirits are responsible for most of the paranormal activity in Fort Monroe. Disembodied voices and the clip-clopping of horses' hooves echo through the casemates. During an investigation of Quarters No. 1, paranormal investigators recorded the voice of a little girl calling for her cat. The deputy of public affairs, Heather McCann, claims that an invisible hand touched her arm during a late-night tour of the fort.

While Fort Monroe may be officially deactivated, it would seem the ghosts there most certainly are not.

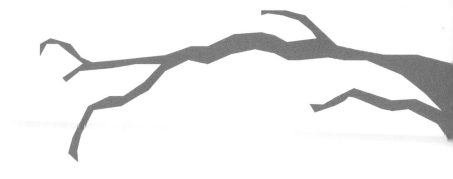

Afterword

It can be said with certainty the American South is filled with intrigue and folklore. Voices from another time and place whisper through its historic buildings and landmarks. Listen carefully, and you may just learn something new, if not totally frightening!

From stories of tragic love to bed-and-breakfasts with too much personality, when you visit the American South, anything is possible!

Dr. Alan Brown is an award-winning professor of English at the University of West Alabama. He has a deep interest in Southern folklore, especially Southern ghostlore and African-American culture and music and has written over thirty books. When Dr. Brown is not teaching or writing, he enjoys reading thrillers and watching movies. He also does a little ghost hunting on the side. His favorite activities, however, include traveling to haunted places with his wife, Marilyn, and playing with his two grandsons, Cade and Owen.

Check out some of the other Spooky America titles available now!

Spooky America was adapted from the creeptastic Haunted America series for adults. Haunted America explores historical haunts in cities and regions across America. Each book chronicles both the widely known and less-familiar history behind local ghosts and other unexplained mysteries. Here's more from author Alan Brown:

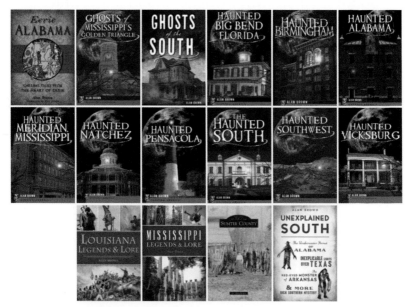